HouSES of SaiNT-TROPEZ

To Robin and Axel

Published in 2004 by
Stewart, Tabori & Chang
115 West 18th Street
New York, NY 10011

Originally published by
Aubanel
An Imprint of Éditions Minerva
A Company of La Martinière Groupe
2, rue Christine
75006 Paris
France

Canadian Distribution:
Canadian Manda Group
One Atlantic Avenue, Suite 105
Toronto, Ontario M6K 3E7
Canada

Library of Congress Cataloging-in-Publication Data
Bariller, Marie.
    Houses of Saint-Tropez / Marie Bariller ; photographs by Thomas Dhellemmes ;
preface by Jacqueline Pagnol ; translated by Paul Hurwit.
        p. cm.
    ISBN 1-58479-388-0 (hardcover)
    1. Architecture, Domestic—France—Saint-Tropez. 2. Seaside architecture—France—Saint-Tropez.
    3. Saint-Tropez (France)—Buildings, structures, etc. I. Title.

NA1051.S25B37 2004
728.8'0944'93—dc22

                                                                            2004007870

Designed by idbleu

The text of this book was composed in Janson and DINEngschrift Alternate.

Printed in France by Pollina - n° L93495

10 9 8 7 6 5 4 3 2 1

First Printing

Stewart, Tabori & Chang is a subsidiary of

Marie Bariller

Photographs by Thomas Dhellemmes

Preface by Jacqueline Pagnol

Translated by Paul Hurwit

HouSES of SaiNT-TROPEZ

Stewart, Tabori & Chang

New York

CoNTENTS HouSES OF SaiNT-TROPEZ

Preface   6

Author's Note   8

THE SwEETNESS OF LiFE   14

16   ODE TO THE SeA
26   IN PeRFECT HARMoNY
34   A REFiNED ARTLeSSNESS
42   LuXE, CaLME ET VOLuPTÉ
52   TiME REGAiNED
64   FaMILY HaPPINESS

VILLaGE RETReaTS   72

74   THE ANSe DE La GLeYE
84   RuE GaMBETTA
90   ON THE RoOFTOPS

DReAMS OF EXoTICISM   98

100   THE PLEaSURE OF ENTeRTAINiNG
108   ON THE SaND
116   oRIENTAL SPLeNDOR
126   AN iNSPiRED ARTisT
136   AN AMERICaN DReAM
146   THE BoHEMIAN LiFE

MEMORiES OF ARTiSTS   156

158   PaUL SiGNAC'S LA HuNE
164   RoMY SCHNeIDER'S SHEEP FaRM
174   CoLETTE'S LA TReiLLE MUSCaTE
180   MaRCEL PaGNOL'S MaZET

AN AiR OF MaJESTY   188

190   INTOXICATiNG GRaNDEUR
202   THE SeA AS ITS NaTURAL ELEMeNT
210   A FLoRENTiNE PaLACE

SAiNT-TRoPEZ, HOME PoRT   220

222   KaRENITA

PRefaCE

In 1963 I learned of the existence of a torpedo factory in Saint-Tropez. My husband, Marcel, and I were searching for a house, a small one, near the sea. La Gaude, where we were living at that time, did not possess the charm of the Var. We missed the Mediterranean and its fishing fleets, dear to Marcel, as well as the mistral, the wind that sweeps away every incarnation of mist and washes the sky. We were also eager to have a place to ourselves so that we could regain the intimacy that had faded somewhat under the slightly intrusive pressure of our families.

I had never been to Saint-Tropez, but the peninsula drew Marcel like a magnet. "There's where we have to go," he told me. He had long been acquainted with Saint-Tropez and had friends there, including the Volterras, who welcomed many artists to their château, and René Clair, who in the 1930s started taking Marcel along on memorable fishing expeditions with the locals.

Good friends alerted us to a *mazet* that was for sale on the Les Salins road. We made an appointment with the owner, a certain Madame Alsina, a charming, effusive Saint-Tropez widow, who said to us: "My husband, who was retired from the torpedo factory, died a year ago. That's why I want to sell and retire to the city." We signed the contract that same day.

It was a small *mazet* with four rooms, surrounded by a grapevine in its death throes that was good only for the verjuice it gave. The dockyards were two steps away. What happiness! Work began the following month. During that long, hot summer we camped out among the rubble.

It was then that we embraced the magic of life in Saint-Tropez—not that of the glittering celebrity nightclubs but the much more bewitching existence of the rue Allard and the market in the place des Lices. We adored the village spirit that predominated there, the funny and genuine people, the markets, the walks in the fading afternoon along the port where we could avoid the crowds. Our excursions led us all the way to Gassin, to Grimaud, or simply to the beaches of Pampelonne and l'Escalet, tranquil, practically devoid of vacationers, where I loved to swim and sail.

We led a simple life: errands run early in the morning, at about eight o'clock, so that we could park without a problem, then the visit to the fish market, to the baker and his brioches, and, lastly, to the Greek fruit and vegetable seller. Sometimes Marcel, always brimming with energy in the morning, would depart alone with a long list of household supplies. He would return two hours later, cheerful and carrying bread, newspapers, notebooks . . . but nothing you could make a meal with! At the same time, though, the trunk of the car was filled to the brim with saws, hammers, nuts, bolts, rolls of wire fencing, and paint cans. In fact, Pétavy Hardware, where he quickly became a regular bursting with the faithfulness of an adept, was the joy of this continually impassioned do-it-yourselfer who slept with only one eye closed. During this period, a small straw hut stood on Les Canoubiers Beach, just in front of the house. The owner's specialties were grilled mussels and Mediterranean prawns, a menu much more appealing than the astounding jumble that filled our car's trunk.

I loved that house because it was so small. Though not very comfortable, it was absolutely charming; the terrace we had built was where we lived, quite literally. The dogs of the neighborhood were our great friends, since we did our cooking on that terrace, and they were only too happy to come share our sustenance. A magpie often settled on the well coping, shaking its head as it called to us. Marcel would answer back with an insult couched in the Provençal dialect.

The jungle of wattle and reeds growing in the garden was a favorite place of Marcel's. He would carve branches he found to make penholders, light in the hand and of the proper size. Not bound by habit, he would write just about anywhere, in the main room but also in the coolness of that terrace, which was shaded by an ancient plane tree.

Evenings were captivating in the company of visiting friends, who differed as much by personality as by occupation: the Bollings; the professor and pastor Valéry Radot, whom his wife called Sioul; the father of that peculiar form of French slang, the magnificent Pierre Brasseur; physician friends from Marseille, Michel Droit and André Roussin, who also owned a house on the peninsula; and many others whom we were always delighted to welcome.

Every August 15 we counted the stars as we lay stretched out on the seaweed that had washed up on the dockyard, and we wished ourselves all manner of good fortune, our petitions escaping upward into the starlight. Have they really come true?

—Jacqueline Pagnol

Author's Note

Tomorrow, we'll have, as we will have the day following that one, too, a day like the day that flows now in a train of blue and golden moments; a day of "stopped time," a day of forgiveness and grace, whose shadows are the favor of a drawn curtain, a closed door, of a fragment of foliage, and not of a sadness suffusing the sky.
—Colette, *La Naissance du jour*, 1928

There are places in the world whose name alone has the power to make us dream, places that for decades have drawn many voyagers, artists, and vacationers. For a privileged few these places become an anchorage, a respite from global travels.

This is the case with Saint-Tropez. Indeed, this Mediterranean peninsula breathes a Provençal perfume that cannot be found anywhere else. A perfume of scandal at times, certainly, heightened by a zestful exhibitionism that is the lodestar of the summer tabloids. This is the Saint-Tropez, shameless alas, that is accessible to all. Yet this small corner of the earth possesses hidden treasures whose subtler, less well-known fragrance emanates from the houses built on its soil. Old wine-producing *mas*, small fishermen's houses, or sumptuous villas, but also ancient sheep farms and majestic châteaux—all attest to a determinedly guarded private life.

By evoking here the intimacy of this small parcel of Provence, a region renowned yet poorly understood, I have endeavored to bring together a multihued bouquet of houses that seem most representative of the world—at once so open and so secret, so grandiose and so simple—of Saint-

Tropez, where the inhabitants prefer to live in a personal refuge that remains, nevertheless, in close proximity to the crowd.

These residences of such varied architecture repose among vegetation that is still wild and tangled with vines. Here the Provençal light, entrancing beyond description, has drawn great painters in their productive primes. Alternatively modest and elegant, displaying an almost princely splendor or inspired by exotic cultures, sometimes surprisingly singular in nature, their diversity accentuates the undeniable enchantment of the peninsula.

As I became acquainted with the home owners, I sensed the extraordinary affection they felt for their houses, each of which asserts its own unique character. Whether built by their forebears or by themselves, or perhaps renovated in more recent times, all reflecting their owner's particular personality and deep desires. Each owner was inexhaustibly communicative about his or her home, recounting its history with an infatuation blended with an equal measure of passion.

These houses, each in its fashion, reveal every inflection of the art of living peculiar to Saint-Tropez: the gracious pace of life unfurls in rustic or highly elaborate gardens, on terraces bursting

with flowers or highlighted by columns, or, again, through the interior decoration, inspired on some occasions by a spirit of profusion, on others by stark, clean lines. Without exception, however, the houses offer a wonderful haven for their occupants, some of whom savor each day the tranquillity their residences harbor, while others come in every season to reenergize for a few days or weeks with family or friends. The children, carried away by their need for space and nature, forge precious memories amid gaiety and laughter.

Each season of the year brings shared moments of happiness, constantly echoed by and

imbued with the colors of this southern French spirit. In autumn, russet vines and fragrant pine forests provide the decor for walks in the surrounding landscape. And while the north can boast of those hearth fires that crackle and hiss during the long winter evenings, how enjoyable it is, too, to lunch on the terrace, allowing the gentle winter sun to caress your cheek!

Springtime enflames the colors of the garden, while the scent of the wisteria looping over trellises penetrates the houses.

In summer, when the Midi sun burns fiercely, the inhabitants take their siestas, dozing to the sound of grasshoppers in the dusk of their shuttered rooms. Then, while the sun is setting, they enjoy feeling the hot sand of the beach underfoot and take in the deep blue of the Mediterranean, rocking gently.

In this way, indifferent to the passing of time, the peninsula continues to work its magic.

—Marie Bariller

THE SWeETNESS OF LiFE

TO LIVE IN AN ETERNAL PROVENÇAL LANDSCAPE, TO BREATHE IN THE WARM, INTOXICATING AIR, TO TAKE REFUGE FROM THE DAZZLING SUN BENEATH AN ARBOR SWATHED IN GRAPEVINES AND WISTERIA, TO DELIGHT IN THE INCOMPARABLE ENCHANTMENT OF THESE HOUSES AGED BY TRADITION, FORMER SHEEP FARMS, WINE-PRODUCING *MAS*, OR SMALL FISHERMEN'S HOMES . . .

THOSE WHO LOVE PROVENCE, WHETHER THIS REGION OR ELSEWHERE, DID NOT LOSE THEIR WAY: THEY HAVE DISCOVERED, IN THESE TYPICAL ARCHITECTURAL CREATIONS WHOSE FACADES HAVE FADED IN THE MIDI SUN, A *DOUCEUR DE VIVRE* THAT THEY JEALOUSLY GUARD AND CLING TO.

IT IS TRUE THAT THESE MODEST HOMES HAVE BECOME INCREASINGLY COMFORTABLE WITH THE ARRIVAL OF NEW GENERATIONS. AND YET THEY HAVE PRESERVED THEIR IDENTITIES, BATHED IN A SERENE HARMONY BORN OF BLESSED MOMENTS AND SHARED INTIMACY.

THE VISITOR LETS HERSELF BE ROCKED BY THE LANGUID, JOYFUL RHYTHM OF THIS ENCHANTING LAND.

ODE TO THE SeA

It was certainly not a whim but, rather, a sign of destiny that guided this man impassioned by sea and sail to what would become his small family island. One spring day he tied up on these rocks like a modern-day Christopher Columbus and found the answer to his question: Would he take to the open sea with wife and children, or would he settle on this strip of land that plunges into the water and build a family haven?

As he climbed the hill, he felt any hesitation vanish. Here he could bring together his love of the sea and a comfortable family life. Because he was a passionate man, he devoted body and soul to the design of his future house. He left nothing to chance, for he was bound to remain as faithful as he could to the spirit of the ancient Provençal dwelling, or *bastide*, a spirit that dictated both proportions and materials.

In his quest for perfection, he built not only the main body of the *bastide* but also the many outbuildings that traditionally distinguish this type of house. Thus, a cow shed and pigeon roost took shape, only to be immediately transformed into rooms; an orangery was built of wrought iron to shelter one part of the swimming pool. This structure, an especially original feature, was designed for use in both summer and winter thanks to a gate that makes it possible to shut off the interior portion of the pool, comfortably heated by a stove of appropriate size.

He shaped the garden by combining the elements most suited to his replica of a *bastide*. Visitors are welcomed by white doves, symbols of peace and harmony, which fly about the aviary, serving as gatekeepers to the garden. Progress through the garden is patterned on a specially designed layout that leads, in turn, to the sudden appearance of an old fountain whose basin holds white and red fish, a fragrant rose garden, then, finally, an appetizing kitchen garden. If the visitor continues, the landscape becomes more dense with foliage. Finally, nature reclaims its authority in the form of a forest of umbrella pines and oaks that falls away gently to the sea.

In the living room, devoted to the sea, a model of a galleon
suspended from the ceiling seems to float in midair.

The sea, which has so deep a hold on this home owner's heart, quite naturally had to make its presence known within the house. For the interior decoration, the master of the house drew his inspiration generously from the fittings of the classic tall ships. The call of the open sea is echoed in each room, most notably through the omnipresence of wood. The furnishings and paneling exude an atmosphere as warm and intimate as that of a ship's hull.

In the spacious living room, which offers views of both the sea and the interior garden, the marine world materializes in collections of colored lamps and terra-cotta figurines of fishermen. A stunning model of a galleon hangs from the ceiling. Binoculars and an ancient telescope make it possible to admire the boats sailing in the distance.

In the main bedroom, which is lined with old paneling, the daylight filtered through the interior shutters evokes the calming half-light of the cabins of sailing ships. The adjoining bathroom clearly signals the thrust of the sea, with its varnished mahogany and skylight.

As a result, against a backdrop of salt air, all of the furniture and objects in this large *bastide* sing in chorus their ode to the sea. Surely, the captain of this beached craft has anchored here for good.

Enthroned amid rustic bric-a-brac, the imposing stove gently heats the orangery that shelters the interior pool, which extends into the garden. By means of a clever gate system, the covered section can be closed off to accommodate guests in the winter as well in the height of the summer.

Scattered throughout the rooms, various collections attest to the master of the house's avid taste for marine objects.

Facing page:
In the kitchen, the sunlight streaming in causes the pendants of the chandelier and the crystal pitchers arranged along the sideboard to sparkle.

Facing page:
In this room, which is completely lined in old paneling, the interior shutters create a gentle
half-light that encourages siestas on summer afternoons.

The skylight and
varnished mahogany
are modern-day
allusions to the classic
sailing ships.

IN PerFECT HARMoNY

In early fall, the first dead leaves dance around the house. Summer and its suffocating heat have vanished, but the gilded light of a radiant sun still enfolds the surrounding countryside. For several years, this beautiful house has known the rhythm of the seasons—since, that is, the family decided to stay in Saint-Tropez year-round. Indeed, the peninsula showers its gifts on those who know how to value it!

Each stage of the year brings new colors and new smells, while the atmosphere and the vegetation are in a constant state of metamorphosis. White and sharp in winter, the volatile light turns to gold in spring, creating soft gray shadows. It becomes orange-yellow in summer, with such harshness that it flattens out the colors and forms dense, black shadows. In the fall the light mellows, making the colors vibrate with the subtle shades it paints.

The grapevines, too, omnipresent in the region, join in the ballet of the seasons. The glowing springtime green of their leaves blends beautifully with the grape clusters of summer. Then the leaves turn russet after the harvests, and fall when winter arrives, leaving bare the small twisted trunks. The house, a locus of perpetual motion, marks the concordance of the natural rhythm with the tempo of family life.

The interior is intended to be changeable, for the mistress of the house likes to move the furniture around to revivify the eye. Some of the furnishings, unearthed during peregrinations among secondhand or antiques dealers, will come to occupy their proper place only several months, or even several years, later.

For all that, though, the interior decoration creates a harmonious whole: comfort and warmth permeate the house, and the decor gives pride of place to family life through its sincerity and lack of pretension—traditional qualities in Provençal homes. This is, moreover, a house entirely aware of its origins: except for necessary additions, which nevertheless maintain the overall proportions and make use of the same materials, the owners drew on the original architecture of this small farm to endow the

The swimming pool seems to have been designed out of respect for the big palm tree.

rooms with the house's singular character. In this spirit, the dry-stone cow shed formed the pattern for a plain, rustic living room. The farmers' former living room, with its low ceiling and dark beams, gives the living room/library a cozy, welcoming atmosphere. Even when they are not original to the house, the other rooms mirror this Provençal state of mind and remain in harmony with the family's natural, convivial lifestyle.

Each of the children's rooms is arranged as the occupant wishes and according to his age: horse posters in one room, photographs of dogs in another, a skateboard and sports trophies in the last. Yet the vast garden surrounding the house is unquestionably the children's true preserve. After school the dogs rush around, as impatient as their small masters to take part once again in their wild races. After a snack that the children consume in one gulp, they launch into their stream of activities: they must go kiss the white pony, say hello to the little ostrich, finish the wooden hut they started the day before. Overflowing with vitality, the children gain in spirit from this benevolent natural world and take daily advantage of the freedom it offers them.

At the end of this autumn afternoon, however, as the light fades slowly and bathes the horizon in a veil of orange, it's time to go inside. The house lights come on, and the children return to their rooms and their schoolwork.

In one hour it will be night, and dinner will bring the small family around the long kitchen table. The dogs, exhausted, stretch out on the warm tiles, sensing that the day is ending. Soon the children will fall into a deep sleep, enveloped by the velvet calm of the surrounding countryside.

*The simplicity of
the furniture, which has
become mottled with time,
harmoniously echoes the
severity of the exposed
stonework of the old
barn's walls.*

One son's bedroom theme is American West in inspiration. A painted wooden fence gate serves as a headboard.

A REFiNED ARTLeSSNESS

A sinuous, rock-strewn road mounts the hill that juts abruptly out of the sea, tracing a route liable to dissuade the casual walker. The hiker's efforts are amply rewarded, however, when she reaches the summit and surveys the imposing panorama. In this spot, the view of the Mediterranean is unique: from this height, the "Great Blue" resembles a gigantic mirror, as if its waves and undulations have abandoned its immense expanse.

The sea's flat, horizontal surface contrasts with the slope and contour of the hill, overgrown with scrub. The blues of sea and sky and the greens of the vegetation sparkle in the ever-shifting light, nature's master of orchestration. In winter, when the trees and plants take on hues of gray, when the lowering sky is reflected in the sea, this magical designer weaves together the disparate elements of the landscape, painting monochromes in silver and slate. The boats in the distance, mere punctuation marks drawn on the immense sea, appear like fragile toys threatened by this fickle element.

Looking down over this disquieting scene, the small house on the hill with its untamed greenery seems alone on the earth. It was built in 1960 for Saint-Tropez natives who yearned for serenity. In the beginning there was only a country cabin without water or electricity, whose only purpose was the repose of its occupants, who came for weekends of leisure. Little enlargement took place during the next few years, but the house did benefit from some cosmetic changes and a number of improvements that made it more comfortable.

Today, a small garden landscaped with flowers and plants native to Provence contrasts with the dense woods that surround it. Tall-stemmed blue irises, lantana with its changing colors, nasturtiums displaying their round leaves and yellow-orange flowers, and roses with their sweet perfume add small strokes of color to the palette of a verdant nature in the heightened manner of an Impressionist canvas. Olive, blackberry, fig, and tamarisk trees wave in the wind, their supple foliage dancing. Walls of a

luminous white set off blue shutters the color of a summer sky. Its humble delicacy modestly asserts itself against the potent natural world encircling it. And yet beneath its manifest fragility, it stands up to rough weather with disconcerting ease. On occasion, the small house even strikes an imperturbably defiant attitude against the violence of lashing winds.

The interior decoration is matched to the house's limited size. No superfluous ornamentation weighs it down. Furniture in unfinished wood or painted blue, small pieces of Provençal flowered piqué, the colored checks of the armchair fabrics—all converge to achieve a simple harmony and inviting freshness in each room. A number of pastel-toned flower bouquets add the final touch. Charm works its magic subtly, delicately.

In the morning, when the warbling of birds wakes her, the mistress of the house opens the shutters in her room to admire a sea made iridescent by the rising sun. She lets her eyes and heart feast on the living canvas that nature paints.

In this house of great charm, the simplicity of the decor emphasizes Provençal arts and crafts: painted furniture, a wing chair covered with a flowered fabric, fresh, elegant prints, wrought iron, and wicker baskets.

LuXE, CaLME ET VOLuPTÉ

How did a small sheep farm a few steps from the sea, near the Château de la Moutte (once inhabited by Émile Olivier, a minister in the regime of Napoleon III), become a house both cozy and opulent? It's probably due to the marriage of Elisabeth and Sebastian, a Frenchwoman and a British native. In every garden niche, as in each detail of the house itself, they have united their two cultures to a single purpose: the creation of a romantic, sensuous atmosphere, resulting in a house and garden that appear to have materialized straight out of a nineteenth-century novel or poem.

The sheep farm, nestled between grapevines and a dense wood of umbrella pines and oak, melts into its natural setting as though dressed in a softly lambent garment, whose tones undergo an autumn metamorphosis from yellowish-green to crimson. Though planted with Mediterranean species, the grounds are designed in the style of an English garden where one can stroll, daydreaming, along its paths. One of these, bordered by lavender and small orange trees in a row of terra-cotta pots, leads from the garden entrance to the house. Another passes beneath a trellis of climbing roses on its way to a small orchard, then to the henhouse, where fresh eggs for breakfast are gathered. First and foremost, however, a majestic avenue bounded by huge umbrella pines slopes gently toward the sea, as though in a gesture of admiration for its beauty.

Scattered throughout the garden are benches that invite the walker to stop and let the landscape penetrate more fully. Set somewhat to the side like a natural pond, the emerald green swimming pool reflects the tall trees around it.

At one end of the sheep farm a large graveled terrace crunches underfoot. Shaded by large pines, it is a romantic milieu, with comfortable ocher deck chairs extending an invitation to indolence. The visitor enters the house through a small entranceway half hidden beneath an arbor of grapevines and wisteria that spreads the sunshine quite nicely into small patches of light.

A majestic
avenue bounded by
tall umbrella pines
descends to the sea.

The interior bears the imprint of Mediterranean culture, even as it asserts its English cottage personality. The lavish yet comfortable decoration confers an air of opulence. For the walls, coverings, and carpets, Elisabeth has chosen warm colors—pale yellow, orange, red—which, when blended with the wood of the furniture and the ecru linen of the deep sofas and armchairs, suggest comfort and hospitality. A table covered with a skirt of old fabric, tall candlesticks, globes of flickering light, the garden roses bowing in silver-plated cups—all are sensuous, elegant details arranged with care by the mistress of the house.

The room that incarnates most fully the spirit of this pleasure-loving couple is, manifestly, the kitchen/sitting room. This is most certainly a room for living in the traditional Mediterranean sense, but above all, a place where spending time is a pleasure, where rusticity is subtly married to elegance. Tall, upholstered chairs surround the long oaken table. Light softened by lampshades vibrates on the golden bottoms of gleaming copper saucepans. Roomy armchairs and a low table frame the stone fireplace. The paintings on the walls and the carpet covering the floor tiles add the finishing touches to a kitchen that breathes the spirit of Epicureanism. In this place the owners love to take their time and to share the sweetness of life with visiting friends.

Through the small-paned French doors shimmering light envelops the countryside. The world breathes in that special end-of-day calm. On the terrace, in a wide wicker basket, stout clusters of grapes harvested from estate vines await the pleasure of the hosts and their guests.

Extending along the facades of the farmhouse, the shaded, inviting terraces promise a salutary calm.

By virtue of its unexpected sumptuousness, its warm tones, its imposing fireplace, and its gleaming saucepans, the kitchen/sitting room is certainly the most innovative room of the sheep farm.

TiME REGAiNED

The visitor is obliged to follow a small dirt road to reach this typical Provençal *mas* set on the edge of the vineyards. Though today the owner sees it as a comfortable family home, it was not always so.

At the time it was built, in 1846, the art of gracious living and decoration mattered little. The structure was intended principally for farming; family quarters were reduced to the bare minimum. Absolute simplicity, even austerity, was the hallmark of its architecture, which was founded on no established aesthetic. In this land of contrasts, the traditional Provençal *mas* had to withstand rough weather conditions: sun and blazing heat in summer, harshness and the weak light of winter, and a frequently violent wind over flat, open country. Such natural conditions left their imprint on farmhouse architecture. Exposure was the key. The house faced southward so as to permit the wintry sunlight to warm the interior. To protect against the summer sun, the substantial thickness of the walls and the shutters, which were kept closed during severe heat waves, retained at least a semblance of coolness. Inspired by the contrast of this precious half light to the dazzling glare outside, Jean Giono reflected: "You enter and the dark envelops you, you stay in this kind of gray pinewood for a minute or two, then the world, the one you know, gradually reemerges."

Over centuries, the desire to fit into the surrounding countryside shaped this building style through the choice of materials as well: exposed vineyard stone for the low walls, ocher tiles for the roofs, and earth colors for the facades.

The history of this *mas* is as typical as its architecture. A story of family and inheritance . . . At the beginning of the twentieth century, the owner had a vast estate devoted to winemaking. At his death the land was divided among his three daughters, each enjoying access to the central well. In fact, the value of any *mas* rose or fell with the water supply available to it.

Facing page:
This covered terrace, once a shelter for pigs, continues to embody the rustic
character of its initial function.

Much later, during the 1960s, a city dweller at the wheel of her Jeep, accompanied by her two sons, discovered the old vineyard *mas* and bought it from one of the sisters. Driven by the desire to lead a country life, she decided to move in, despite the extensive work the house would require. She preserved the plain outward appearance of the farm but renovated the interior as her tastes dictated. She placed prime importance on the comforts the house so sorely lacked, and assigned to each room a use different from what was originally intended. Without diluting the original Provençal spirit, she created a true home.

A shelter once intended for pigs has kept its stone trough, but has since become a pleasant shaded terrace. Old waxed tiles cover the beaten earth that forms the floor of the cow shed; it is now a large sitting room incorporating a monumental oak fireplace. And the winepress? It's now a country kitchen that still retains the small openings through which the grape bunches were fed into the vats. On the second floor, the old hay barn has been divided to create an office/library that encourages meditation, and the master bedroom has been decorated with Napoleon III furniture and portraits of the family ancestors.

Years have passed since the renovation of the *mas*. But its Provençal austerity continues to attract one of the owner's sons. Returning to the smells and memories of his youth, he comes to refresh his spirit for several months out of every year in this house devoid of artifice, a home in which time seems to have stopped at a period of profound happiness!

The kitchen was laid out inside the old winepress. Beams and chestnut-colored furnishings exist in decorous harmony with the tiles, which have been polished to the point of looking like leather.

Each room contains objects and furnishings of iron and wood,
materials of a past time that coexist harmoniously.

Portraits of ancestors on walls painted the color of faded roses and Napoleon III furniture infuse this bedroom with an agreeably antiquated atmosphere.

FaMILY HaPPINESS

Nothing predestined this modest fisherman's shack to become a welcoming family home. It all started in 1941, when Monsieur and Madame D., a young married couple, decided to buy a vacation home in the French Midi, even though they had no idea of location and their budget was decidedly meager. It was then that Monsieur D. asked his mother to go out in quest of some rare jewel. A highly skilled violinist, Mama was an intimate of the artistic set, which was drawn during that period to a certain small village on the Mediterranean. Saint-Tropez's fame was beginning to spread, and Mama's search naturally focused on this wild peninsula. After many fruitless trips, she finally came upon a fisherman's house on Les Graniers Beach, not far from the sailors' cemetery. When the young couple visited this little house containing three tiny rooms, and without running water and electricity, they succumbed immediately to its charm. The sale was quickly made.

Every summer, the house would come alive for two months. The family expanded and the children grew. In the very early morning, when the silver sea was burnished with an oily patina, they would often descend onto the deserted beach to water-ski. The rest of the day slipped joyously by, suspended between sand, sea, and sun. With the advent of evening, everyone returned to the house to wash their salt-encrusted skin on the well coping. As night fell, they lit the kerosene lamps; then, comfortably settled on the narrow terrace, they savored the moon's reflection floating on the sea at their feet. With the children asleep, one hears only the sound of the waves gliding endlessly onto the sand.

The D. family lived in this way until the mid-1960s. The lack of space and comfort in no way diminished the affection they felt for the house. Still, as the children grew older, the pinched space became a burden. It was time to make a decision.

At this time, the son was finishing his architectural studies. Who could be better equipped to design an extension of the house without altering its character? Drawing inspiration from the small villages of Greece, for which he has a special fondness, he designed six small, separate rooms lining a narrow passageway. The original house, left unchanged, would be the stage for the family's common activities; in the narrow kitchen, for example, weekly menus are written on small slate boards. Amid a cheerful disorder, each family member participates in his or her own way in preparing dishes redolent of familiar Provençal fragrances and flavors.

Today, the great-grandchildren brighten up summer days, when four generations reunite in a spirit of genuine well-being. Despite the imposing residences that surround it, the small fisherman's house has remained the most comforting of homes for this family, which treasures the simple happiness it has bestowed on them for so many years.

Facing page:
Beyond the terrace trimmed with wild reeds,
Les Graniers Beach is visible.

Not so long ago, the
well was the sole source
of water for the cottage.

*Divided
into separate
bungalows, the
rooms, with their
simple, unaffected
decor, welcome
travelers on
holiday.*

VILLaGE RETReaTS

WHEN THE VISITOR ENTERS A VILLAGE HOME, SHE IMMEDIATELY IMMERSES HERSELF IN THE CURRENT OF A REGION'S HISTORY. SHE BEGINS TO DREAM AND IMAGINE HOW LIFE WAS LIVED HERE CENTURIES AGO. SHE IS TRANSPORTED BACK IN TIME THROUGH THE PORTAL THAT THESE ANCESTRAL BUILDINGS PROVIDE. WHETHER LORDLY RESIDENCES, PRIVATE MANSIONS, OR SIMPLE FISHERMEN'S HOUSES, THEY ARE ALL WITNESSES TO A TIME THAT HAS VANISHED. CERTAINLY THEIR WALLS COULD RECOUNT NUMEROUS ANECDOTES AND FAMILY HISTORIES.

THESE HOUSES REMAIN THE TRUE ROOTS FROM WHICH THE MEDIEVAL VILLAGES SPRANG; THEY ARE THE PROTECTED INHERITANCE IN WHOSE VERY CORE THE TUMULTUOUS FLOW OF PAST EVENTS TOOK PLACE. EVEN IF TIME HAS FORMED A GLOSS OVER THEIR FACADES, THESE VILLAGE RETREATS REMAIN THE GUARDIANS OF THE MEMORY OF THE PENINSULA.

THE ANSe DE La GLeYE

"This is one of those charming and simple daughters of the sea, one of those modest little villages rising up from the water like a seashell, nourished by fish and sea air and producing sailors. . . . Here are the smells of the fishing trade, of smoldering tar, sea brine, and hulls of boats. Here the scales of sardines shine like pearls on the paving stones." With these words, writer Guy de Maupassant describes in his travel narrative *Sur l'eau* his feelings on his arrival in Saint-Tropez in 1887 aboard his boat, *Bel Ami*.

This evocation of a small fishing port limns a peaceful existence that unfolds in the rhythm of days at sea and the mending of nets. But if you go back still further, you will find that, for centuries, the inhabitants of Saint-Tropez fought valiantly to repulse enemy attacks launched from the sea. For this reason, at the end of the fifteenth century the villagers protected their town with ramparts designed as a deterrent and flanked by a tower at each corner. The first, which was erected in the middle of the port, has for the most part disappeared. On the opposite side, to the south, rose the Jarlier Tower; a portion of the wall that originally sloped downward to the Old Tower is preserved at the sea's edge. By walking along the shore you reach the fourth tower, called the Portalet Tower. Between these last two towers, round and proud, you find the Anse de la Gleye, a neighborhood named for the first church in Saint-Tropez, which was built on the shore. In this district, houses were built in the Genoese style, their colorful facades crowded against one another in perfect alignment, with a superb view of the entrance to the gulf.

Closest to the water, huddled on the rock that must fend off the roaring waves in rough weather, are three fishermen's houses, which were made into a single residence during the 1960s by a family in love with the old town.

The innovative character of the house, which derives precisely from this three-to-one overlapping arrangement, finds its greatest expression in the entangled staircases that, independently of one another, connect the various rooms within a labyrinth full of surprising twists.

An attractive arched doorway sculpted in wood and framed by stone lintels leads to a small, somewhat darkened entrance hall. An upholstered bench and two imposing chandeliers stand guard. Then, through a double wooden door, you proceed into the dining room: painted crimson and adorned with a formal marble fireplace and furniture made of polished wood, its comfortably middle-class air contrasts with the simplicity of the building as a whole. The ground floor contains a pretty, classic living room into which light streams through large windows looking out onto the sea. This room opens onto a beautiful stairway that incorporates a wrought-iron railing, and the steps lead, in turn, to a covered terrace, a kind of "blue sitting room" designed to match the hue of the sea.

When, during the first days of October, under a gray-tinted sky with highlights of mauve, dozens of sailboats, both old and modern, gather for the famous "Sails of Saint-Tropez," the family has prime seats for this enchanting ballet, watching as the sun breaks here and there through autumn's heavy clouds. When the sky is clear, however, and the summer days are kindled by bursts of sun, an uncovered terrace built into the roof allows sunbathing in total privacy. The terra-cotta floor and the ocher cushions lining its settees harmonize with the coloring of the roof tiles and the facade. You feel a sweet daydream taking shape inside you. Even though the smells of the fishing fleet are now gone forever, and engine-powered yachts have replaced the old wooden-hulled boats, the medieval town still reveals its charms to lovers of the past.

When the houses were merged, several staircases were built to join rooms that had originally existed separately.

A Moroccan sitting room, with its vaulted ceiling, has taken shape in the old boathouse.

The wooden door, featuring a fish knocker, opens onto a
narrow entrance hall, where tiling extends halfway up the walls.

The stately dining room adorned in red breathes an air
of classicism seemingly out of place in a fisherman's home.

RuE GaMBETTA

In the rue Gambetta, formerly the rue du Puits-de-la-Ville in the heart of Saint-Tropez, a number of beautiful private mansions were built in the eighteenth and nineteenth centuries for powerful ship owners and wealthy merchants. General Allard lived for a time in one of these magnificent residences, which dates back to 1835. The scion of an ancient Saint-Tropez family, Allard rebuilt one of Napoleon's armies before being named commander in chief of the forces belonging to the king of Lahore. Wishing to settle his family in his native village after an absence of sixteen years, he received permission from his commander to return to France. As fate would have it, though, he was obliged to return to Lahore before he could even begin to enjoy life again on the peninsula. As an important figure in the history of Saint-Tropez, Allard's bust sits both at the entrance to the town and at the rear of the garden adjoining his former house.

Early in the twentieth century, the mansion was deemed too large to be preserved in its original state and was divided into apartments. Then, in 1950, a family with its roots in Lyon moved to Saint-Tropez. Dr. R., a newly licensed surgeon, set up practice at the entrance to the village. A number of years later he founded the Oasis Clinic, offering the peninsular population medical services that had previously been lacking.

The doctor and his family took one of the apartments in the old mansion, and their lives settled into the sequestered rhythm of the village, where, perhaps not surprisingly, the arrival of "foreigners" under the disbelieving eyes of the natives began to sow chaos during the summers. After the birth of six children, however, the family felt hemmed in. Dr. R. then bought the other apartments in turn . . . and the spacious residence regained its former splendor. Today, the mistress of the house can give free rein to her passion for antiques, which she uncovers whenever her travels take her throughout France and Portugal. She brings back imposing pieces, such as a massive oak console table covered with a marble top, or wide armchairs and tall sculptures.

All of these furnishings are arranged in the long hall that, in a masterstroke of design, connects the entrance to the glass door of the interior garden. The pieces leave their noble imprint on the hall, which is further accentuated by a wall tapestry, a colorful chandelier, and heavy crimson hangings.

Portraits of the family's children adorn the majestic staircase, draped with a long, stately red carpet. The rooms above are furnished with sculpted wooden beds and decorated with chandeliers made of Murano glass, which enhance the air of the baroque that predominates in the house.

One of the family daughters evoked the Christmas celebrations of her childhood, when the house, lit by sparkling garlands of lights and the soft illumination of the chandeliers, provided an aura of grandeur and ceremony—wondrous memories forever engraved in the family consciousness.

While today none of the brothers and sisters live in the house, they return regularly, both physically and in spirit, for weekends or longer vacations. Spurred by both faithfulness to the past and the desire for peace, they desired to preserve the integrity of their superb home. They did, however, build a swimming pool in the interior garden, over which a handsome, thick olive tree stands guard atop its pedestal.

Here, in a calm disrupted only by the sounds of the wind in the tall trees, you have difficulty imagining that, just a few steps away, a crowd mills along the narrow streets and through the port in the airy, joyous, cheerful effervescence of summer.

The imposing furniture and statues of sculpted wood,
the fabrics of glowing red and soft carpets, make this house an
extraordinary spot in the very heart of Saint-Tropez.

ON THE RoOFTOPS

Planted on one of the wooded hills of the peninsula, the small village of Ramatuelle boasts a distant, and unobstructed, horizon. On summer days, this tranquil village comes to life with festivals, whose renown attracts lovers of jazz and theater. And at aperitif time these floods of fans congregate on the place de l'Ormeau, on the shaded terrace of its charming café.

This medieval village stamped with Provençal tradition harbors many other treasures too. Their secrets lie far back in history, for beneath its peaceful appearance, Ramatuelle has experienced suffering inflicted by multiple waves of attacks. It bears deep scars from the painful period of Arab occupation in the tenth century. A number of tangible traces persist, including, for example, the Saracen Gate. Most notably, though, the village derives its name from this period; according to some historians, the Arabs called it Rahmatullah, or "Divine Providence."

Following Provence's liberation at the hands of William the First, the village architecture underwent a transformation. The inhabitants erected high walls around the houses, which backed up against one another along narrow, winding streets. Among these, one residence stood out from all the others: the Château de Ramatuelle, which occupied the entire center of the village, was home to the seignorial families that lived in succession until the seventeenth century. It was at this time that, with the reunification of all parcels of land making up the feudal estate, François Félix d'Audibert became lord of Ramatuelle, a title his descendants retained until the French Revolution.

Although renovated many times during the centuries, the château's high walls still stand imposingly over a small paved square blooming with bougainvillea. After mounting the several stone steps polished by time, the visitor reaches the perron, where a large gray cat appears to keep watch. A heavy wooden door opens onto a darkened entrance hall. A healthful coolness reigns inside, thanks to the thick walls of the structure.

In the dim half-light, a small country kitchen gives off Provençal fragrances—simmering tarragon and garlic—while soft music escapes from the second floor. Taking a staircase that extends upward in a fairly straight line, the visitor emerges into an impressive sitting room. Once your eyes have adjusted to

the light flooding in through the immense windows, you're able to take the full measure of this monumental room, rising to a dizzying height and fitted with a mezzanine, where an office and library are ensconced. From that vantage point, you have a magnificent view of the sea. Other rooms of comparable stature have been converted into separate studio apartments for family members and friends.

Yet it's by mounting a small spiral staircase that you come out upon the most enchanting spot of all: an expansive terrace that hangs suspended over the whole village. The panorama spread out at your feet appears to materialize in all of its pictorial detail from a painterly universe, recalling Cézanne's descriptions of the villages of Provence: "red roofs against the blue sea." From this perch, indeed, the roofs of the houses, which seem molded to the precipitous contour of the hill, look like the steps of a long, irregular staircase descending to the sea. You're overwhelmed by the sense, at once illusory and palpable, that you could touch the church bell tower, an intense yellow in the sunlight and so close that it seems an invited guest on this improbable terrace. The picturesque village reveals its very heart in the charm of its ancient stones.

In the late
afternoon, as the
sun grazes the
hillside, the
Ramatuelle bell
tower appears
to invite itself onto
the terrace.

The height of the sitting
room ceiling is so imposing that
the mistress of the house has built a
mezzanine beneath it. Vestiges of
the old ornamentation, restored
during recent renovation, adorn the
slope of the staircase.

DReAMS OF EXoTICISM

UNDER THE BURNING SUN OF THE MIDI, WHEN THE QUIVERING LIGHT IMBUES EVERYTHING WITH ITS PURITY, THE PINES AND OLIVE TREES INHABIT AN UNDULATING LANDSCAPE. BEACHES ARE STRETCHED IN LONG CARPETS OF WHITE SAND, WHILE THE ROCK-STREWN STREAMS ARE HIDDEN AWAY IN THEIR WILDNESS. MANY ARE THOSE WHO HAVE BEEN PERSUADED THAT THEY HAVE FINALLY FOUND A UNIQUE PLACE IN WHICH TO SETTLE. STILL, THOUGH, THEY HAVE NOT FORGOTTEN THE MANY COUNTRIES THEY HAVE TRAVELED THROUGH AND LOVED. UNDER THE INFLUENCE OF THEIR PASSION FOR TRAVEL, THE RESIDENTS OF SAINT-TROPEZ HAVE REPRODUCED IN THEIR HOUSES AND GARDENS THE ALLURING SPIRIT OF DISTANT CULTURES.

AFTER SCOURING THE SOUTHERN ARCHIPELAGOES, VISITING CALIFORNIA, OR SETTING OUT TO DISCOVER SOUTH AMERICA, THEY HAVE FREELY FUSED THEIR DREAMS OF EXOTICISM WITH THEIR LOVE OF PROVENCE, THEREBY CREATING A TIMELESS, ECLECTIC AMBIENCE.

THE PLEaSURE OF ENTeRTAINiNG

Hospitality could be the watchword of this long white house close to Tahiti Beach. The mistress of the house, its very soul, has the gift of putting you at ease from the first moment. She loves to entertain, and it shows. Quite probably, consideration for others was the impetus for her entry into the world of theater. In more than twenty-five years she has produced a great many plays, while extending to all who have known her a boundless sensitivity and generosity. In this place, her conviviality informs even the architectural decisions, most notably the layout of the house.

It was on this beautiful plot in 1965 that Monsieur and Madame C. decided to seek the services of an architect, Monsieur Chauvin, for the construction of a spacious villa modeled on the Spanish hacienda. Their single-level home encompasses, behind wide windows, a succession of large rooms bathed in light. Monsieur and Madame C., both sun worshipers, pursue our presiding star continuously throughout the year. As soon as the cold invades northern Europe, like migratory birds they take off for warmer climes. From Madagascar to the Caribbean, from Polynesia to the Seychelles, they sail among the islands as winter follows winter.

They bring back magnificent shells, pearl necklaces, and vividly colored paintings by folk artists, which they add to their proliferating collections at the house in Saint-Tropez. This abundance of exotic objects enriches the atmosphere of welcome and warmth they have created here.

Madame C. has thought of everything necessary to entertain her guests to the fullest. She has carefully arranged and furnished charming rooms that open onto small, cool patios, where her guests can find peaceful solitude at siesta time as the sun blazes over the swimming pool. At the aperitif hour, her friends gather on the long terrace bordering the sitting room to regale themselves with a well-cooled rosé and heaps of appetizers.

The villa, built on one floor, opens along its full extent onto a long, parallel swimming pool while, simultaneously, it enjoys an unobstructed view of Cape Tahiti.

Arranged so as to suggest small sitting rooms, a few armchairs and delicate settees are spread across the terrace. Their 1930s style woven rattan gives the place a retro, colonial appearance. While the sea, set in its frame of umbrella pines, sparkles in thousands of small dots of light recalling the pointillist paintings of Paul Signac, Madame C., attended by her two pugs, arranges dinner on the patio that adjoins the sitting room. Seated around the sophisticated table, the guests delight in the calming, mellifluous lapping of the fountain. As the evening festivities continue deeper into the night, invariably a music lover will take his seat at the white grand piano and spread enchantment through the warm nocturnal hours.

A passionate woman, Madame C. loves nothing more than to share these moments of release, which she orchestrates with a kind of beneficent magic. Antonin Artaud could be speaking for her when he wrote, "What could prevent me from believing in the dream of the theater when I already believe in the dream of reality?"

The terraces possess a colonial look, due in large part to the old rattan settees and armchairs purchased during the couple's many travels.

Numerous souvenirs of voyages have been arranged around this room, in which the eighteenth-century Portuguese wooden bed is surrounded by vividly colored Peruvian folk paintings and shell necklaces from the islands. The two pugs are in command, like true masters of the house!

ON THE SaND

On a white sand beach shielded from the winds, not far from La Moutte, lies a modern, square white house built in 1931 by Marie Bonaparte, a descendant of the emperor's brother. She was ahead of her time: in 1926 Bonaparte, a patient and friend of Freud, numbered among the twelve founders of the Société Psychoanalytique de Paris. This woman of refined taste dreamed of a home at the water's edge, where she could meditate far from the city's hubbub. At a time when crowds had not yet invaded the coast, she bought this property from shepherds and built a small one-story house with a flat roof. The design of the house was Cubist in inspiration. She gave it the name of a rare plant that grows among the dunes: Lys de Mer, or sea lily.

Many years later, Monsieur de H. was searching for a spot that would recall the stubborn wildness of his native Brittany, and though the property lay in a sunnier, milder climate, he fell under the spell of this most original of dwellings.

The very quintessence of dreamlike reality emanates from the surrounding landscape. In front lies Les Salins Beach, its fine sand spun out to an infinite horizon by the luxuriant Mediterranean. And behind is a salt pond rimmed by bamboo and wattle, where the shimmering light of the setting sun suggests the native accents of Africa.

Monsieur de H. had dreamt of a garden that would bloom in the sand. After numerous difficulties he managed to grow olive trees and plants suited to the coastal climate.

As a lover of architecture, he endeavored to enlarge the house while preserving—and, in fact, accentuating—its geometric forms and acute angles. He chose to increase the ground-floor surface area in order to keep the house on a single level. But the most spectacular architectural feature lies in the immense picture windows, which to retract completely into the walls, removing any barrier between house and nature.

Facing page:
From the rooftop terrace, one may enjoy sunrise over the sea,
then sunset over the salt pond located on the property's edge.

At night, the moon hanging in the immensity of sea and sky bathes the house's interior with its faint metallic glow.

In the large sitting room, with its white walls and wooden floor, the furnishings play on a theme of simplicity. Sofas upholstered in white cotton and armchairs in natural rattan that can easily be moved outdoors reflect a desire for an unencumbered life of complete flexibility. Vivid, intense colors echo throughout the house: yellows, blues, and crimsons set off the immaculate white, which becomes incandescent in the sunlight.

This fresh, vivifying atmosphere evidences the dynamic character of the owners. At any time of day, they need only push open the small wooden gate to step onto the beach for volleyball games or to reach the sea on which they windsurf. This energetic family could not have found a more beautiful decor for its sports activities.

We may ask: Are we in Corsica, on the Brittany coast, or on one of the Caribbean islands? This architecture, free of any obvious Provençal tradition, and the wild landscape it is set in erase all landmarks and reference points, giving the house its singular character. A sublime perfume of exoticism predominates here.

The white-painted wooden floor was chosen for its warmth and tactile comfort. The furniture, easy to live with, can be moved inside or outside at whim. Additionally, all four sides of the sitting room are open to nature.

oRIENTAL SPLeNDOR

When discussing architecture, people often speak of "integrating into the site," a principle that implies a respect for the environment, and a concern for harmony with the nature and culture of a particular place.

This house, built on a hillside overlooking Les Graniers Beach, fully implements this architectural concept. As a Saint-Tropez inhabitant to the very core for nearly thirty years, architect Roger Herrera could hardly have designed his residence any other way. While searching for inspiration in this steeply sloped site, which offers the expansive views of the Gulf of Saint-Tropez, Herrera absorbed the essence of the surrounding countryside before choosing the form of his future residence. The town's citadel, with its angular battlements and hexagonal tower, sparked and sustained his creative enthusiasm. This late sixteenth century monument, an incontestably hieratic emblem of military might, was the well of inspiration for his building. Herrera constructed long stone walls duplicating the citadel shapes, bounded by cut off corners and sharp edges; these were the foundations designed to support the upper stories of the house.

Wishing to take full advantage of the extraordinary panorama, he rejected the idea of enclosing the rooms with conventional walls. What better material than glass to allow torrents of light to penetrate and to enable the inhabitants to feast on the encircling landscape? The oblique facades of the hexagonal pavilions that house the bedrooms offer a wide prospect on the landscape and the sea. The bathrooms, too, were founded on the principle of interaction with nature: the views from the bathtubs, set into slabs of Burgundian stone, are magnificent.

Paradoxically, the use of natural materials imparts a substantive delicacy to the entire house, for a sense of detail plays a primordial role. Materials and geometric shapes play off each other, creating a pervasive harmoniousness from one room to another.

The furnishings and decorative objects, the products of various civilizations, display the architect's love of travel: Byzantine mosaic tables, ancient world maps, a reclining Buddha, and chairs from China.

Herrera has seamlessly extended the interior's essence into the grounds. The garden seems to have sprouted spontaneously on the ruins of some ancient fort. Greek earthenware jars, like archeological vestiges lend a certain rhythm to the terrace, whose wrought-iron guardrails, twisted and irregular in shape, appear to have suffered and survived the insults of time.

The spillover swimming pool, or "horizon pool," as Herrera prefers to call it, gives the impression of a natural pond flowing into the sea—an illusion amplified by the gulls that settle there from time to time. One of the palm trees, its trunk bending toward the blue water as though hunched under the weight of years, is reflected on the pool's incandescent surface.

This villa embodies a subtle mingling, a magisterially wrought association of what has been weathered and what is contemporaneous, of the primitive and the refined, a house of glass rising from the ruins and an appealing glance at the history of Saint-Tropez, whose citadel attests to four hundred years of history.

The twisted railings creatively delineate the contours of the house. Below, the sailors' cemetery of Saint-Tropez is visible.

Greek oil jars guard the octagonal rooms with their fully glassed-in walls.

Each room is designed to offer a sweeping view, from the bedroom decorated in Asian style to the bathroom, whose stone bathtub, built into a floor of Burgundian slabs, overlooks the sea.

The world of travel is omnipresent, from the Murano glass flutes, to the ancient maps of the world in the living room, to an old Chinese chest and an Indian birdcage transformed into a light fixture hanging in the entranceway.

AN iNSPiRED ARTisT

When an artist looks for inspiration, with all his senses alert he lets himself be guided by his emotions. After leaving his native Switzerland to travel the world, Muggiasca sought in vain a piece of land that could persuade him to settle. When he crossed the dense, wild forest on one of the hillsides in Gassin, however, he felt himself transported by signs that could not lead him astray: the yellow mimosas along the rutted road, the blue-tinted eucalyptus bordering the land, the unique light that, for one hundred years, had inspired so many masterpieces, the sky so blue and so clear in that light.

Fascinated by color, Muggiasca has always painted large flat surfaces from which crosses, eggs, and arrows, primitive forms to which he is viscerally attached, emerge with expressive clarity. With the close collaboration of the architect François Vieillecroze, he designed his house as a work of art. He gave free rein to his imagination as he reconciled his desire for modernity, his attachment to wood, and his love of intense, warm colors—truly the dream of an artist. Thus, a house of striking originality reflecting the full measure of his aspirations took shape.

Inspired by his travels in Mexico, Muggiasca maintained his taste for simple structures and unfinished materials, at the same time creating the large space typical of artists' studios. From the entrance, a long, high-ceilinged hall with walls painted in a brilliant yellow (his preferred color) transports the visitor into the universe of the owner. The artist's state of mind is boldly announced! In an act of inspiration, he employed the high walls as so many outsized supporting pieces, upon which he could express his passion for color. He took pleasure in making yellow, orange, and fuchsia dance on a background of wood tinted lightly with a sandy beige stain, on walls coated for the most part with this same beige, and, finally, on the polished gray concrete floor. Neutral colors thus become illuminated by the blaze of these three vivid colors, which emit their warm breath throughout the house. The artist's wife shares this same inspiration, and personally dyed the fabrics to perfectly match the decor.

The egg-shaped swimming pool overlooking the Gassin hills is stirred by the evening breeze.

There are few doors here; instead, spaces are left substantially open. Two mezzanines protected by guardrails hewn from tree trunks form pendants at each end of the immense living room. The terrace, designed with an eye to unity, plays on the same opposition of forms and colors: the gaps between the boards that cover it allow stunning plays of light. Like imaginary paint-brushes, the rays of the sun draw short-lived, contorted sketches on the long yellow pillars and the wide table made of fuchsia-colored concrete. Close to the house, cactuses highlight a pervasive South American influence, pointing the way toward a waterfall flowing mellifluously into an egg-shaped swimming pool.

This house, a three-dimensional artwork of exquisite stylistic cohesiveness, showcases Muggiasca's talent for composition and color. All that's left is for the Midi sun to add its light and intensity, playing with shadows through the course of the day.

The textural walls, vivid colors, and different species of cactus everywhere evoke Latin America.

The brilliant yellow of the walls accentuates still further the monumental feel of the entrance, which extends upward to a dizzying height.

From the bath to the bedroom, warm tones and rounded shapes predominate. The sculpted wooden varanus lizard and the hearth opposite the bed carry us away to Mexico.

AN AMERICaN DReAM

The August day promises to be hot and bright, yet the blazing sun goes wonderfully with this large pink and white villa, designed by the architect François Vieillecroze, which unfurls its opulence in a style reminiscent of Hollywood.

On this summer morning, when the freshly mowed lawn is still wet from dew, the white-and-pink-striped cushions have not yet been placed on the chaise longues, and an abundant breakfast has been arranged on a table set up outside. An air of softness and indolence prevails. No trace of last night's party remains. The house, perfectly immaculate, is ready for the new day. One by one, the family members and their guests gather around the large table.

You might suppose that this scene comes right out of a movie. Everything here alludes to the American dream. A long zoom shot . . . The wide perron framed by small palms leads to the double entrance doors made of light wood. Once inside, your eye is drawn immediately to the infinite depth of field of the landscape, barely veiled by the immense sliding picture windows.

Wherever your eye rests, the suave colors of the decor heighten the impression that you have walked into a film shot in Technicolor. Against a milky-white background, candy pink—the color of choice of the master of the house and his daughter—flirts harmoniously with a lively anise green. The living room, white and spacious, welcomes us with its long sofas, deep floral-print armchairs, and the dazzling smiles of family and friends in portraits astutely arranged.

The expanse of the terrace, which extends the entire length of the living room, is broken up by white columns and bowls of flowers. On the other side lies a deep green lawn. Is this the seventh art or reality? A young man crosses the grass toward a large pool house. On the terrace, shaded by tall climbing plants, he sits in a wide white wicker armchair, unfolds a magazine, and brings a glass to his lips.

Not far away, while the bright sun illuminates the verdant scenery like some fabulous projector, a young woman and her son, soon to be joined by a couple, take their places beside the swimming pool covered in pink mosaics. The child jumps cheerfully into the clear, tepid water. The long beach of Pampelonne and the sea stretch out before them. Like an exclamation point, the Camarat Lighthouse lends a final note to this magnificent production. Two small white dogs play, running zigzags around numerous palm trees of all sizes. Tearing down the twisting path edged with banks of lavender, they burst into a huge field of olive trees planted in three orderly rows. In the evening, as the sun sets and the lights in the garden come on, their distorted trunks and gray foliage rival in grandeur the palm trees, with their straight trunks and slender leaves.

As the air softens on this summer evening and the enchantment of the lights spreads a mood of tranquillity over the villa, the family and its many guests savor the mellowness of this American dream, transposed to the Saint-Tropez peninsula.

On one side of the
house, palm trees of
all kinds and luxuriant banks
of flowers ornament an
impeccably groomed lawn.

Swathed in light, the swimming pool with its pink mosaics surmounts the expansive Pampelonne Beach and the iridescent sea beneath the burning summer sun—a magnificent vision, so Hollywood.

Green and pink predominate in the house, from the spacious living room to the terrace adjoining the pool. The harmonious color scheme is echoed in the deep sofas, the cushions of the deck chairs, and even the orangeade glasses and tea service.

THE BoHEMIAN LiFE

The sky, a deep blue tinted with mauve, gradually clears at the horizon. A slight breeze brings a cooling freshness and rhythmically stirs the needles of the young pines, while a pinkish glow announces the coming day.

In this wild landscape nature uses, and overuses, its freedom of expression: tall reeds rise on the property's boundary, and wild grasses march over it as they wish. No garden here.

Beams of light filter discreetly into the house. The coffee, dripping heavily into the coffeepot, disturbs the silence, a disruption taken up in turn by the chirping of a few birds perched on the two blackberry bushes in front of the small house. The smell of coffee spreads through the house and teases the noses of the sleeping inhabitants. This is how Peter awakens on this beautiful summer morning. One of his great daily pleasures is to get up early to absorb those magical moments when the sun appears in a sky filled with fluid, pure colors, then to slip outside for a long, solitary walk.

Taking one of the many paths leading to Saint-Tropez across the pine forest or along the beach, Peter never ceases to discover new vantage points. His chosen route leads him to the port where, settled on a terrace, he joins other early risers in taking full advantage of the fragile calm. On market days, he interrupts his conversations to rummage through the stalls, looking for a piece of furniture, a drawing, or a fabric he can find a home for in his house. This simple tenant farmer's home, which at one time housed animals and a wine vat, has been transformed by his skill into a multicolored nest, a model of bohemia.

You enter the kitchen through a narrow glass door; several small rooms follow like strung pearls each vying to be the most charming and cheerful. The vivid colors of the fabrics, cushions, and kilim carpets—on which you walk barefoot—stand out against a background of floor tiles and wooden furniture. The old wine vat, whose thick, cutout wall delineates a beautiful curve, serves as a sitting

Facing page:
Sheltered by vines, the arbor adjoining
the house encourages conviviality.

room, but definitely an unconventional one, furnished only with a mattress covered with fabric and soft multicolored cushions that fill up the entire width of the narrow room. Peter likes to use it to welcome friends who show up unannounced to savor, among other dishes, the delicious crumble made by this native Englishman and inveterate traveler.

It was quite probably in India, his family's longtime country of residence, that Peter acquired his taste for bright, shimmering colors. The small bedroom adjoining the house, built into what had formerly been the henhouse, embodies the home's enduring spirit. With its curved Thonet wood and bed nestled into an alcove and supported on a platform, a small rattan chair, and numerous color-print fabrics, these sleeping quarters constitute a whimsical nod to the past. Here, the heady odor of incense permeates the air, just one further detail inspiring the evocative name Peter has used to christen the room: the Happy Hippie Room! A small terrace, hidden under an arbor on which the grape clusters take on a blue cast in late summer, captures on certain evenings the look of the Orient; heavy cushions on the ground, massive hangings suspended from the arbor, and lanterns with their orangey glow confirm the persistence of an imperturbable life force.

At all hours, this simple, colorful house and its wild landscape conjure the mellow, bohemian spirit of the 1960s.

Facing page:
Colors happily clash throughout the house.

Trunks, mosquito nets,
kilim rugs, and vividly colored
paintings add an electric energy
to the bedrooms.

Facing page:
The curved scrollwork of the wooden bed, beach robes hung from the ceiling, and pink walls
have inspired the name of Happy Hippie Room, at one time a humble henhouse.

*The bohemian spirit flows from room
to room, especially in the sitting room, with the
beautiful curve of its thick wall.*

MEMORiES OF ARTiSTS

ART HAS UNDOUBTEDLY BEEN THE FORCE THAT REVEALED TO THE WORLD THE INCOMMENSURABLE BEAUTY OF THE PROVENÇAL MEDITERRANEAN. ITS INCOMPARABLE COLORS, ITS COUNTRYSIDE WHERE "THE VEGETATION SINGS EVERY-WHERE A FRENZIED HYMN IN PRAISE OF THE SUN," FIRST CAPTIVATED WRITERS IN THE MID-NINETEENTH CENTURY. SUBSEQUENTLY, PAINTERS SENSUOUSLY AWARE OF THE LIGHT OF THE MIDI USED THEIR CANVASES TO PARSE THE EMOTIONS AND SENSATIONS THAT THIS LAND INSPIRED IN THEM. THEY IN THEIR TURN DREW ADDITIONAL WAVES OF ARTISTS AND WRITERS TO THE PENINSULA.

SUBSEQUENTLY, PROVENCE THE INCUBATOR OF REVERIE ATTRACTED ENTERTAINERS, FILMMAKERS, AND STARS, WHO HEIGHTENED THE NOTORIETY OF THIS SMALL CORNER OF PARADISE.

LET US NOW OPEN THE DOORS TO THESE HOUSES AND PLUNGE INTO THE WONDERFUL LIVES OF THOSE ARTISTS.

PaUL SiGNAC'S LA HuNE

Could we possibly evoke Saint-Tropez without mentioning the artist who, through his talent, left his mark on the history of painting and of the town?

A man enamored of freedom, a passionate admirer of the sea who was initiated into sailing by the painter Gustave Caillebotte, Paul Signac, "painter of seascapes and sailor among painters," arrived here in 1892 on his sailboat *Olympia* by way of Marseille and the Midi Canal and anchored in this small fishing port. He became infatuated with the countryside, and with the light that his friend Henri-Edmond Cross had boasted of. Signac soon met the painter Auguste Pégurier, a native of Saint-Tropez, who introduced him to the peninsula's charms. The artist had no doubts: "I'm not just stopping over, I will live here!" He rented a modest cottage at the edge of Les Graniers Beach, five minutes from the town. "Secluded among the pines and roses, open to the golden banks of the Gulf . . . here I have enough to keep me working as long as I live. Happiness is something I have just recently discovered." He duplicated on his canvases the fascinating sea light, which inspired numerous masterpieces, such as *L'Orage*, *Voiles et Pins*, *Saint-Tropez*, and *Le Quai*.

Five years after his arrival, the artist bought a house overlooking the beach, which he called La Hune (Crow's Nest). He enlarged the living quarters and built a huge studio with a view of the sea.

The house was surrounded by beautiful grounds planted with grapevines, whose wine Signac esteemed greatly, and fragrant orange trees lining a stone wall. He planted many trees—including eucalyptus, blue pine, and plane trees, which have since grown tall—that flirted with the sun, throwing their shadows against the facade of the house. Blue irises and African lilies swayed on their long stems around the perron. In the aviary, today neglected, pheasants, hens, and turtledoves coexisted in a cheerful cacophony. And in the heart of the garden, cats, which the painter adored, came and went with muffled steps, never disturbing the painter's concentration.

Facing the garden, the perron gives access to the living room, whose shutters remain halfway closed on hot summer days. On the street side, Signac's studio, with its wide arched windows, opens onto the Mediterranean seascape.

During that period, Signac encouraged many artists and friends to share in his awed admiration for the peninsula: Henri-Edmond Cross, of course, an habitué of Le Lavandou, and also Henri Manguin, Albert Marquet, Pierre Bonnard, Charles Camoin, and Henri Matisse, who spent the entire summer of 1904 in Saint-Tropez.

It was here that Matisse made the rough sketch of a major work, titled *Luxe, Calme et Volupté*, alluding to the Baudelaire poem "L'Invitation au Voyage." This magnificent canvas is now displayed at the Musée d'Orsay in Paris. Infatuated with the painting, Signac bought and hung it in the dining room that he had just enlarged, saying: "On this panel backlit between the two windows, you have created luminous and shining harmonies."

In this way, the artist re-created a world that pictures the sensations his painter friends were experiencing amid the Provençal landscape. Signac would later return to this light-permeated scene of creative fermentation, which the talent of Signac himself and his fellow painters reconstructed with such mastery in numerous immortal works of art.

The house exhales a subdued, somewhat austere atmosphere, in which time seems arrested at the period when the renowned painter lived here.

RoMY SCHNeIDER'S SHEEP FaRM

Romy Schneider, a woman whose presence stirred emotions, a magnificent actress with a spellbinding vocal timbre, found in this house a refuge that fully met her need for space and nature. Released from professional constraints and doubts, Ms. Schneider, her hair drawn back under a scarf, her face unembellished and radiant, experienced here her most carefree moments, surrounded by family and close friends, whom she welcomed without affectation, her mind at ease, her body refreshed, giving herself up completely to the sun beside a pool decorated in green mosaics. In this refuge from the eyes of the world, she could devote all of her care and attention to her son David and cherish her daughter Sarah, to whom, in fact, she had given birth in Saint-Tropez.

Beyond the property's boundaries, the eye becomes lost in a sea of greenery. The hills wooded with oak and dense pine, the domain of boar and fox, and the small valleys where vineyards predominate form the backdrop against which epiphanous moments can be lived out. This vast property in complete harmony with the surrounding countryside is doubtless what entranced the new owners, as it did Romy Schneider herself. A few fruit trees—apricot, fig, and almond—scattered over the grounds, beautiful oleander hedges, and a number of slender cypresses are the only tangible signs of a human will to tame nature. In places, the garden is wild enough to enable the children to play at being Robinson Crusoe without fear of damaging it. Accordingly, they don't hesitate to build huts, modeled on a very idiosyncratic architecture!

Enlarged over the years, the old sheep farm with its sunbleached facade mirrors the surroundings through its rustic construction and the simplicity of its decoration. While the interior has changed somewhat since the actress lived here, the current occupants have preserved the fullest possible harmony with the pastoral grounds, whose thoughtful yet carefree style is the essence of its charm.

RoMY SCHNeIDER'S SHEEP FaRM MEMORiES OF ARTiSTS

The pale, faded tones of the furnishings and fabrics, along with the bleached beams, endow the rooms with a gentle, lustrous atmosphere that enfolds everything in a touching overlay. In the living

room, which opens onto the dining area, two wide, capacious off-white sofas accord well with the washed-out yellow Provençal armoire, the faded pink carpet, and the long, patina-rich country table. The fireplace, often lit even on summer evenings, and the colorful candles underscore the comfort and tranquil ambience of this house, which remains inviting in all seasons.

Indeed, the decor, at once simple and intimate, unapologetically makes use of unfinished materials, such as the polished gray- and beige-tinted concrete in the kitchen and some of the baths. The bedrooms, too, resonate—note their delicate shades of ecru and almost monastic spareness—with the sobriety and serenity of this enclosed world.

In this plainspoken interior, however, one room stands in pointed contrast to the others by virtue of its surprising luxuriousness—the bathroom of Ms. Schneider herself, which has remained unchanged over the years. With its bathtub and basin carved in pinkish beige marble, this is the centerpiece, the most intimate room of the house, the one that leaves the visitor with a palpable image of the woman and of the actress.

RoMY SCHNeIDER'S SHEEP FaRM MEMORiES OF ARTiSTS

A mellow coolness prevails in this small corner of the terrace, sheltered from meddling curiosity.

Inside the house, the beams and woodwork have been painted white.
The washed-out colors and the painted Provençal furniture imbue the rooms
with a romantic, carefully ordered insouciance.

Romy Schneider's massive bathtub, hewn from a block of marble, loses its formal character when the children enliven it with their games.

A guest bedroom, decorated with monastic spareness, opens directly onto the garden.

CoLETTE'S LA TReiLLE MUSCaTE

Once you're inside the grille of the blue gate, the owner comes to greet his guest on a path shaded by an arbor of greenery and flowers, leading to a house of faded pink brick. Colette's legendary home, which a family from the Tarn purchased in 1941, has preserved the charm of days gone by, as well as the simplicity so cherished by the writer, whose posthumous presence still permeates the entire home.

When, during the mid-1920s, Colette discovered "maritime Provence," she fell immediately in love with Saint-Tropez and its peninsula, deciding on the spot to buy a house there.

Set a little apart from the village on the Les Salins road, she came across "a modest little farmhouse with low ceilings and a terrace awash with wisteria." She became delighted with the way "the sea borders it . . . enchanting this plot of land with a light-permeated shoreline" *(La Naissance du jour)*. Colette immediately renamed it La Treille Muscate, an allusion to the Muscat grapevine that winds around the well.

From 1926 to 1939, Colette stayed for several months at a time in this house, whose intriguing facets she never stopped describing: the garden, the sea in proximity, the lights, the scents—all wellsprings of the emotions that she shared with her readers in her books.

Colette ordered her days here according to a well-defined ritual, for day after day this sensuous woman wished to savor each magic moment offered to her. She loved to awake at dawn to drink in "the instant when the blue sky begins to rise from the sea." She happily spent the greater part of the morning in gardening, an activity that "links inseparably the eyes and mind with the earth." The land that she cherished was planted with vines, a small pinewood, a few fig trees, mandarin orange trees and sunflowers, dahlias and rosebushes, and a kitchen garden sown with tomatoes, eggplant, mint, and tarragon. Then arrived that magic hour when she swam in the aquamarine-shaded waters off Les Canoubiers Beach, next to the house.

176 CoLETTE'S LA TReiLLE MUSCaTE MEMORiES OF ARTISTS

There she joined friends who were as enamored as she of the white sand and intransigent sun: the painters Andrée Dunoyer de Ségonzac, Luc-Albert Moreau, and André Villeboeuf; the violinist Hélène Jourdan-Mohange; or the critic Gignoux, whom she often kept over for lunch, where they delighted in the Provençal dishes she loved: green melons, anchovy paste, stuffed scorpion fish, and eggplant fritters, everything accompanied by a "cool rosé" from Saint-Tropez.

Then, while the "grasshoppers sawed away the midsummer days in short bursts," Colette went upstairs for a nap in her bedroom with the shutters closed. "Let him throw a stone at me who has not experienced the desire to sleep on a hot midday in Provence."

Upon awakening she sat down, her back to the garden, at her worktable, which she was careful to position in the corner of a small room "a little dark, not very comfortable, turned away from the enchantments of the sea." And she inscribed her work on the blue background of the pages. Silence and the austerity of the decor were the best possible companions of this woman, who wrote: "Only in this sun-swept country can a heavy table, a straw chair, an earthenware jar brimming with flowers, and a dish with its inner edge engulfed in enamel make up the whole of a furniture arrangement." At nightfall, she laid her mattress on the terrace outside her bedchamber and went to sleep, comforted by the nocturnal freshness.

During this entire period, Colette never tired of Provence or of its inhabitants, with their beautiful manner of speaking. She cultivated here both her home and her friendships, occupying her hands with gardening and her mind with writing. This balance in her life fulfilled her, nourished her, and kept her perpetually alert, probing nature, animals, and human relationships. "A life of wild luxuriousness, barefooted, a faded wool shirt, an old jacket, a lot of garlic, and swimming at all hours."

Facing page:
The terrace adjoining the small kitchen has retained the charm of former times.
It mirrors the Provençal way of life that the writer prized so greatly.

To the front of Colette's bedroom is the small terrace where she loved to fall asleep in the refreshing Saint-Tropez nights.

MaRCEL PaGNOL'S MaZET

The name Marcel Pagnol conjures up, immediately and in a rush, the highly colorful images of the distinct character of Provence: an arid land, a blazing sun, a girl with long blond hair, grasshoppers and their mocking song, a singsong accent, a heavyset man in a white sleeveless T-shirt . . . Each of Pagnol's books and films plunges us happily into the Provençal milieu, the inexhaustible source of his inspiration and backdrop for his prolific output.

His deep-seated attachment to the country of his youth also affected his personal life. In fact, the writer periodically felt the need to return to Provençal landscapes, which he surveyed during long hikes in La Treille, near his hometown of Aubagne, and in La Gaude.

Less well known was his attraction for Saint-Tropez, which he discovered in the 1930s. He spent summers here for ten years, after he and his wife bought, in 1963, a small *mas* near the village a few steps from the sea, on the Les Salins road. The wattle and reeds on his property supplied him with his most beautiful penholders.

Pagnol, animated by an immutable passion for the water, fell in love with this *mazet*, which had three wells in the garden and on the small terrace. Jacqueline and Marcel decided to enlarge the house by adding a long room with arched windows, in which the artist set up an office facing the radiant countryside. Above the office, a large terrace welcomed sunbathers and Ping-Pong enthusiasts. In this peaceful haven Pagnol also built a workshop as an outlet for another of his enthusiasms: do-it-yourself projects. Dressed in old trousers and sweaters, which he called his "house uniform," and shod in canvas espadrilles, he liked to welcome his friends informally around a barbecue.

Although very close to the wild life of Saint-Tropez, he felt at peace and protected, as he wrote to his friend Father Calmels, inviting him to visit: "You'll live sheltered from the dangers of this world. L'Estragnet is not a place of damnation. It's my cloister."

This decor "à la Pagnol" was the factor that, several years later, captivated two Parisians in search of sun, the cicada's song, and serenity. They found in this house the ideal context in which to live the life free of artifice that they sought.

A descendant of the renowned geographer Paul Vidal de la Blache, the new owner, a dealer in secondhand goods and antiques, viewed Pagnol's *mazet* as the hoped-for spot where furniture and objects mottled by time would find their natural place. The couple fashioned an eclectic, highly colorful, cheerful

decor designed to appeal to children and to friends who would come and go in this "house of good fortune," as everyone agreed to call it.

The freshening shade of a guardian plane tree wraps the small terrace transformed into a veranda, which contains a novel dining room whose walls are built of exposed stone. In the middle, the well now finds itself incorporated into the decor, a rather quaint pedestal for flowers and candles.

The bedrooms, too, manifest this desire for open spaces, as well as the soothing bohemian atmosphere that penetrates the entire house. In the huge master bedroom, built in the space formerly occupied by the old terrace on this floor, a zinc weathercock presides over a roulette wheel from a casino in Cannes, which lies in front of paintings arranged at floor level, beneath windows framed by red curtains that are frozen in their angled posture by simple knots. The diaphanous mosquito net over the bed and a wooden African sculpture strike a note of exoticism. Close by, globes of all sizes crowd the shelves, like reminiscences of the illustrious family ancestor, and which calls to mind this thought of Pagnol himself: "One attains the universal by staying at home."

A roulette wheel from a Cannes casino, paintings arranged on the floor, and red curtains held with simple knots create an eclectic decor in a corner of the sitting room.

Adorned with an overflowing library, Pagnol's old office has become a studio.

Facing page:
With its magnificent mosquito net, colorful carpets, and African sculpture,
the master bedroom emits an exotic perfume.

One of the
bedrooms on the
second floor
displays a
plenitude of color
amid a cheerful
jumble.

AN AiR OF MaJESTY

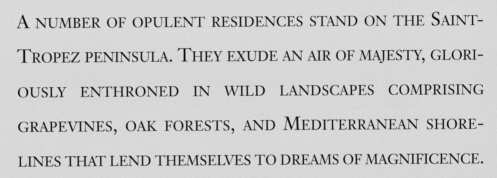

A NUMBER OF OPULENT RESIDENCES STAND ON THE SAINT-TROPEZ PENINSULA. THEY EXUDE AN AIR OF MAJESTY, GLORIOUSLY ENTHRONED IN WILD LANDSCAPES COMPRISING GRAPEVINES, OAK FORESTS, AND MEDITERRANEAN SHORELINES THAT LEND THEMSELVES TO DREAMS OF MAGNIFICENCE.

RISING PROUDLY ABOVE THIS COVETED LAND, THEY RECALL THE PLUSH BAROQUE SPLENDORS OF TUSCANY; OR THEY EMBODY A MODERN, AUSTERE SOPHISTICATION—UNLESS, OF COURSE, THEY FLAUNT SURFACES WORN TO A PATINA BY THE YEARS OR ADOPT THE POSTURE OF AN IVORY TOWER WHOSE BASE FENDS OFF THE SEA'S PERSISTENCE.

EACH HOUSE BEARS IN ITS OWN WAY ITS LOFTY RESPLENDENCE, SET OFF BY THE COLORFUL GLOSS OF THE LIGHT STUDDED WITH GOLD, WHICH ELEVATES TO ITS FULL MAGNITUDE THE SENSUOUS PLEASURE OF THIS LANGUOROUS LAND.

INTOXICATiNG GRaNDEUR

Sunlight and blue air shrouds the Château Volterra, hanging like an eagle's nest on the summit of a hill, surveying in its magnificence the Bay of Bomporteau and Cape Camarat. Pink porphyry from the Estérel was quarried to build the château, a late-nineteenth-century transposition of a Tuscan castle to the French Mediterranean. It rises proudly to confront the sea, its gaze fixed on at the Hyères Islands and the remote Alps—a captivating panorama in a unique site; in short, a magical place.

This edifice was the very special gift that Léon Volterra, founder of the Lido and the Casino de Paris, offered to his wife in 1926. Simone Volterra, with her generous heart, immediately opened the doors of her sumptuous residence to the inhabitants of the region, while cheerfully welcoming many artists, including Raimu, Maurice Chevalier, Charles Vanel, Marcel Pagnol, Colette, and so many others who made château life a succession of gilded hours. Upon her death, Madame Volterra bequeathed the immense property to her adopted children. However, the château remained unoccupied for several years, solitary against the sea.

When he arrived at the estate, the new owner, in thrall to his new domain, decided to bring back its once animated lifestyle. First and foremost, he re-established estate winemaking, which had been severely damaged by years of neglect. He consulted the best winemakers to learn how to produce an extraordinary product worthy of its provenance; with extreme care, he replanted vines on a special plot within the vast estate. Having decided that quality would prevail over quantity, he combined traditional production methods with modern technology, which dictates that every stage of production be rigorously controlled. He first created a rosé fully consonant with the Provençal tradition, then went on to whites and reds, which he made it a point of honor to render especially distinctive.

Besides the vineyard, the property also encompasses a huge, wild park that slopes away to the shoreline and a number of rocky creeks. In contrast, the vegetation around the château has been

transformed into a well-delineated, elegant garden in which romantic, intimate lanes skirt beautiful banks of flowers.

The visitor enters through a huge glass and wrought-iron door, a foretaste of the refinement of the decor. While externally the edifice is massive, almost imposingly so, the entirely refurbished interior remains airy and delicate, owing to the successful fusion of classic materials and resolutely contemporary furniture.

Not far from the entrance lies the immense kitchen, the ne plus ultra of a room for actual living. To better adapt the residence to modern life, the owners have removed a great number of small service areas in order to create, beneath a high vaulted ceiling, a single huge room that promotes serenity as well as an open-heartedness emanating in part from its light-toned furniture, light-colored fabrics, and walls painted a luminous beige.

This same air of tranquillity and restfulness predominates in the vast living room. Subdued somewhat by long ecru curtains, the sun spreads rays shifting light over the white wooden floor and the wide linen sofas and chairs. Color plays a vital role in the rooms' decor, giving to each its own distinct personality. The particular character of each of the many rooms, all of which offer stunning views of the Mediterranean, can be attributed in large measure to its color scheme, whether it uses dynamic contrasts or harmonizes elegantly in composed monochromes.

The Château Volterra has finally regained its former pride, and a promising future beckons. Its owners can now reopen it to the artistic life, including exhibitions, performances, and evenings worthy of a past with which the reborn edifice has come to terms. In this coastal landscape, which each day at noon trades its iridescent hues for a deep blue, the warm sun enfolds this majestic residence, blushing like a shy young girl.

Santolina sculpted into balls, slim cypress, and olive trees at the border marked by a stone wall: this garden offers in sophisticated fashion the symbols of Provence.

In one of the sitting rooms, wide armchairs upholstered in linen frame the stone fireplace, which is ornamented with the Volterra seal.

Facing page:
Beneath its vaulted ceilings, the immense kitchen breathes a softness inspired by monochromes in beige and ecru.
The sink, sunken into a thick stone slab, strikes a note of modernity.

In this bathroom with its generous proportions, the bathtub carved from stone and the exposed shower in the middle of the room exhibit a luxurious minimalism.

The linen curtains, the bed, and a dressing room in natural oak add soft, caramel-colored highlights to the master bedroom, permeated with a resolutely contemporary spirit.

THE SeA AS ITS NaTURAL ELEMeNT

Following the coast toward Saint-Tropez, passing the tip of the Cape of Saint-Pierre, you come upon the pretty Les Canoubiers Bay, whose undeveloped beach is edged with tamarisk and wattle. A tall, imposing tower rendered in a contemporary style seems to keep watch at the entrance. This building, seemingly fortified, is in fact one of the most outstanding of the private villas built in Saint-Tropez during the 1950s.

During that period Baron Van Opel, a German manufacturer of automobiles bearing the same name, and his Colombian wife asked a Marseille architect, Monsieur Margaritis, to design a house in an innovative style as close as possible to the water. Lover of the "Great Blue," the owner dreamed of a home hanging suspended over the waves. The architect's first design delighted the couple, though their perfectionist inclinations prompted them to modify the original plans many times . . . and it was in this intensely exciting atmosphere that the long building process began.

Construction of this splendid residence seemed especially never-ending because the builders were working at a time when modern construction methods did not yet exist. No fewer than thirty workmen dug and swung pickaxes to erect, inch by inch, this strange villa. The reinforced concrete tower, with its slight curvature toward the sea, built with an overhang, attracted attention all around like some haughty grande dame. A dozen stonecutters were charged with fabricating on site an attractive facing of Mougins stone.

His passion for the sea unabated, the master of the premises next built a boathouse and a small private harbor to make his childhood dream complete. Finally, after seven years of construction, the stunning house was finished, baptized with the charming and evocative name Tour et Voile (Tower and Sail).

THE SeA AS ITS NaTURAL ELEMeNT AN AiR OF MaJESTY

Many years later, on a hot July day, a small boat moored to the tower rocked gently, patiently awaiting a cruise at sea. Benign wavelets brushed the stone wall with a hollow lapping. This was the kind of enchanting vision that had prompted the owners to purchase Tour et Voile; now, in their turn, they were taking delight in the Mediterranean surging at their feet and parading its many colors, whose varying

tones and hues Van Gogh trumpeted: "You don't always know whether it's green or purple, you don't always know if it's blue, for one second later the unsettled light has taken on a shade of pink and gray."

The sea is the omnipresent motif extending even to the house's core; it seems to form the fluid backdrop of the spacious rooms, which project onto it the translucence of their long picture windows. In the tower, which houses bedrooms and an office, as in the huge dining room and living room in the left wing, the effervescent sea is incorporated into the decor.

The modernity and pure lines of the decoration graciously bow to the beloved Mediterranean's influence. Even the nicely landscaped green patio, sheltered behind the house from the sometimes violent mistral, seems to have abandoned all hope of outdoing the sea in splendor. Standing proud and upright, this house, a modern fortress built in praise of the sea, allows the iridescent marine hues to wash voluptuously over it.

A line from Baudelaire has a strong resonance here in this house: "Free man, you will always cherish the sea."

Facing page:
The dining room, in its elegant simplicity, permits the Mediterranean to preside over its table.

Below:
The kitchen could serve in a great restaurant with its large, professional
stove and long, mobile sideboards.

Everywhere, the eye is unfailingly drawn to the omnipresent sea—
in the cool bedrooms, in the white living room with its clean lines, and in
the huge tower office.

The long custom-made desk clings to the curvature of the tower. Built facing the sea, it summons soothing thoughts of the water.

A FLoRENTiNE PaLACE

Planted over dozens of hectares, Provençal grapes mold pliantly to the contours of the peninsula. Their ephemerally colored leaves and bluish clusters hang heavy over the landscape on the immense Bertaud-Belieu estate. At the beginning of the modern era, the grape grew wild, yet it owes its renown to the Romans, who cultivated it and produced here the great vintages of antiquity. The barbarian invasions trampled the winemaking region into ruin; only with the coming of the Middle Ages would the trade again take hold in Provence. This was the epoch that saw the creation of the Bertaud estate, which, up until the French Revolution, encompassed the Belieu smallholding as well as its vineyard and house.

Not until the 1930s did this country house built within the confines of the village of Gassin became a luxurious villa fashioned in the Florentine style by Sir Charles Noël, a devoted admirer of Tuscany, who entertained the political elite of the time at spectacular receptions. Despite fairly extensive changes made to the house in the following years, its successive owners preserved, and even accentuated, its magnificence, making it truly an Italianate extravagance.

Upon gaining access to the property, the visitor is immediately wonderstruck by the grandiosity of the long, graveled entrance avenue edged with olive trees in full bloom and enticing grapevines. You enter the house by one of two staircases that swing wide around a stone fountain sculpted into a gaping shell. Welcome is extended by two neoclassical statues, placed near the entrance door, before you are plunged into an almost theatrical, unanticipated, richly decorated world. In the cool half-light that characterizes Provençal houses, you see materializing gradually before you the furniture from widely diverse periods, all the best of its kind: a grand piano with wood inlay, wing chairs scattered in the small, intimate sitting rooms, sparkling chandeliers, gilded, intricately wrought mirrors—all elements triggering lightshows that create a magical iridescence in the reception rooms.

Facing page:
Backed up to the house, the glass sunroom wrought in ironwork is cradled
by the surrounding plants and flowers.

Shouldering up to the house, a beautiful wrought-iron and glass sunroom opening onto a superb park serves as a summer salon. Gigantic trees—eucalyptus and palm several hundred years old—cast their seemingly limitless shadows over an impeccably kept lawn. Tall statues of women of a sensual grace populate this Garden of Eden. When seen from the swimming pool, which is disguised as an ancient ornamental lake, the monumental residence takes on, behind its long ocher facade and green shutters,

the classic air of a wealthy matron.

And yet, beneath its opulent sophistication, the decor cultivates an eccentricity marked by humor and a nimble gracefulness that become apparent, most notably, in the many bedrooms full of wit and originality. The decoration in each is inspired by a specific motif, but all achieve a wonderful balance among period furniture, colorful hangings, lace, and delicate furnishings, along with the amusing trompe l'oeil designs that adorn the walls and ceilings. You might think these bedrooms had been assembled from stage scenery; for that reason, they inspire gentle daydreams in the visitor.

This shining extravagance reaches its peak in the luxurious indoor pool. Modeled on the Roman baths, it seems to have escaped from some fantastic dream, with its slender columns in the antique style, its frescoes representing bath-inspired scenes, and its wide armchairs set around the immense stone hearth. The crystalline water, illuminated by a shaft of light from the glassed-in ceiling, highlights this dreamlike atmosphere. The exuberance suffused through the entire villa induces a lightness of spirit. The visitor lets herself be carried away by the emotions stirred by this house, this dream of a Florentine palace.

In summer, the long ecru awning over the veranda welcomes the soothing light.

Facing page:
Baroque and unconstrained in spirit, this attic bedroom with its massive beams
surprises and charms with its theatrical decor.

Facing page:
This bedroom, with its heavy drapes, canopy bed, and walls ornamented
with moldings and trompe l'oeil paintings, cleverly recalls the grand spirit of
the seventeenth century, which also informs the adjoining boudoir.

SAiNT-TRoPEZ, HoME PoRT

YOU MEDITERRANEAN, TEMPERAMENTAL, WARM, AND SENSUAL SEA, WITH THE LUXURIANT SHADES OF YOUR PALETTE, WITH COLORS SOMETIMES DEEP AND INTENSE, OTHER TIMES TRANSLUCENT, YOU CRADLE VISIONS OF ETERNITY AND THE INFINITE. FOR CENTURIES, YOU HAVE BEEN A HARBINGER OF CATASTROPHE BUT ALSO A FOSTERING, HEALTH-GIVING MOTHER FOR THE INHABITANTS OF THESE SOUTHERN COASTS.

WOULD MAUPASSANT AND SIGNAC HAVE YIELDED TO SAINT-TROPEZ'S CHARMS, WOULD THEY HAVE PORTRAYED IT WITH SUCH DEEP FEELING, HAD THEY NOT DISCOVERED IT FROM THE SEA? THIS SMALL FISHING PORT, ONCE SWARMING WITH THE PROUD BOATS OF TIMES GONE BY, THE *TARTANES* AND POT-BELLIED *POINTUS*, NOW THE ANCHORAGE OF MODERN, OPULENT YACHTS, STILL WELCOMES THE BEAUTIFUL CLASSIC SAILING BOATS MADE OF WOOD AND BRONZE, WHICH UNFLAGGINGLY RETURN TO BREATHE THE AIR LADEN WITH MARITIME STORIES OF THEIR HOME PORT.

KaRENITA

The story of this beautiful sailboat endowed with clean, slender lines began in 1929, in a Massachusetts boatyard where it was christened. Designed by the celebrated naval architect John Alden, it sailed off to an extraordinary destiny, passing successively through years of grandeur and oblivion.

In the mid-1930s, Errol Flynn, a Hollywood movie star and passionate lover of sailboats, became enthralled by the twenty-three-meter ketch. Though considered by many sailors to be bad luck to change a boat's name, Flynn renamed her the *Sirocco*, and undaunted by this superstition, set sail for a cruise along the Atlantic coast. Some years later, in 1942, after numerous passionate and tumultuous incidents, he parted with the boat, which slipped gradually into oblivion, its marine hardware and interior plundered. Years passed with it in this disgraceful condition . . . until the day when a man driven by discovery and legend heard of this two-master beached pathetically in a small boatyard on a Caribbean island. He bought it as soon as he set eyes on its slender lines. In the early 1990s he restored its original name, as if to exorcise any looming evil destiny. The *Karenita* then began the adventure of its resurrection.

Gradually, its new owner and several devoted friends went in search of the original plans and scoured antiques dealers and auctions to recover the components of its marine hardware, which had been scattered throughout the Caribbean. The most skilled artisans rallied to the cause: they rebuilt the boat's mahogany interior, restoring its clean lines, its teak deck, its tall, hollow masts made of Oregon pine, and its varnished teak cockpit and tiller. Through perseverance, the *Karenita* experienced a gradual rebirth; when it was returned to the water, gleaming and majestic, it seemed that the years of decline had vanished from memory.

The boat then headed for Europe, where it took part in numerous prestigious races reserved for classic sailing craft: it won the Palma, Porto Cervo, and Imperia competitions, and several weeks later triumphed at the famous Nioulargue in Saint-Tropez. The village then became its home port.

Of course this sailboat, with its athletic lines and its wind-filled sails slices through the sea at exciting regattas. Yet, for all that, it remains an elegant cruising vessel, eminently suited for peaceful sailing in warm, clear Mediterranean waters.

When the sun sets, the swells of the sea smooth out, and the water becomes tinged with gold, the crew anchors in some hidden creek for the night. The crew members, reimmersed in sensations recalled from youth, fall asleep, exhausted by wind and sea spray and rocked by the lapping of water against the hull. In the early morning, the sea, in the guise of a silver lake, invites them to dive. They swim around the boat, whose lofty masts seem to pierce the eternal blue of the sky.

Now, though, the crew raises the anchor and lifts the sails, which snap sharply in the wind to the accompaniment of the clinking of the winches and the tapping of the snap hooks and grommets. The sailboat moves far offshore, trailing its wake as it heads toward new horizons, captivated once more by the spectacle of the shimmering sea stretching to infinity.

Every convenience has been thought of, including this stove mounted on universal joints
so as to allow the onboard preparation of meals that unite the crew in conviviality.

The map table and
the measuring instruments
in the navigation room.

Far from diminishing the air of refinement,
the constricted space of the cabins enhances the delicate
gingerbread style of the varnished mahogany.

BiBLioGRaPHY

Blanc, Jean-Jacques Jelot, *Pagnol inconnu*, Éditions de la Treille/Michel Lafon, 2000.

Bonini, Émmanuel, *La Véritable Romy Schneider*, Pygmalion, 2001.

Bonnaure, Jean, *Si Ramatuelle nous était contée des origines à nos jours*, 1994.

Bourgeron, Jean-Pierre, *Marie Bonaparte*, Presses Universitaires de France, 1997.

Calmels, Norbert, *Rencontres avec Marcel Pagnol*, Éditions Pastorelly, 1978.

Colette, *La Naissance du jour*, Flammarion, 1928.

de Germond, Jean-Daniel, *Saint-Tropez, Le Temps retrouvé*, Équinoxe, 2000.

Goujon, Michel, *Saint-Tropez et le pays des Maures*, Hachette, 2000.

Massot, Jean-Luc, *Les Maisons de Provence*, House Book/Éditions Eyrolles, 1997.

Musée de l'Annonciade de Saint-Tropez, Catalogue, Éric Hild / Musée de l'Annonciade, Méditerranée, De Courbet à Matisse, Catalogue de l'exposition, Réunion des Musées Nationaux, 2000.

Pagnol, Jacqueline and Ferrari, Alain, *La Gloire de Pagnol*, Institut Lumière/Actes Sud, 2000.

Perron, Claude, *Saint-Tropez, Réhabilitation de la ville ancienne (relevés, notes, croquis)*, Office Culturel et d'Animation de Saint-Tropez, 1981.

Rosati, Joseph, *Saint-Tropez à travers les siècles, Études historiques*, Les Amis de la Citadelle, 1991.

AcKNOWLeDGMENTs

I wish to think all those who were at my side and supported me during the entire process of the creation of this work, most notably the owners of the houses, who so kindly opened their doors and gave me their confidence.

A thousand thank yous to Thomas Dhellemmes, who was able to capture the singular nature of each house, and who bore my anxious moments with humor.

Thank you to the entire team at Éditions Aubanel, and especially to Anne Serroy, who believed in this project and watched over me while allowing me a great deal of freedom; and to Agnès Busière for her effectiveness and enthusiasm in the face of everything.

I would like to extend my boundless appreciation to Jacqueline Pagnol for the warm welcome she gave me.

I feel deep gratitude to my family and friends, who listened to me talk many times about this work so close to my heart.

I would especially like to thank Michèle Bariller for her unfailing help, her invaluable support, and our life-saving fits of laughter. I tenderly thank my children for their patience and encouragement. Thank you, too, to Patrick Khayat for allowing me to discover and develop a love for Saint-Tropez several years ago.

Thank you to Serge Normant for his wise suggestions and unshakeable friendship, to Gérald Cohen for his sound presentations and critical sense, and to Marie-Anne Faure-Lachaud, who quite spontaneously introduced me to Thomas Dhellemmes.

A very great thank you goes to François Vieillecroze for his repeated support and cheerful friendship, and to Roger Herrera for being available.

I wish also to thank Michel Wegelin, Abraham Cohen, Joseph Baronco, and Frank Boumendil for the doors they opened for me, and to Alain Ferrari for his recommendations.

Thank you, too, to Madame Raboutet of the Saint-Tropez Archives, and to Monsieurs Innocenti and Gourmelon for their invaluable information.

Thank you to Gilles Martin-Raget for his beautiful photographs of the *Karenita* at sea.

Finally, I wish to express my gratitude to all of the architects, both famous and unknown, who have for centuries built these houses within which life is such a great pleasure.

—Marie Bariller

I wish to thank Valérie Duport, to whom I owe my love for Saint-Tropez. It was there, in fact, that I married her in 1995, on Pampelonne Beach.

I would like also to thank Aimery C., my assistant, who photographed the Colette house while my daughter was being born.

Thank you, finally, to Olivier Conan, Laurent Beauvais, and Patrick Khayat for their hospitality.

—Thomas Dhellemmes